THE HISTORY OF EXPLORATION
MAGELLAN
& THE AMERICAS

NEW
FOREST
PRESS

Publisher: Tim Cook
Editor: Guy Croton
Designer: Carol Davis
Production Controller: Ed Green
Production Manager: Suzy Kelly

ISBN: 978-1-84898-299-4
Library of Congress Control Number: 2010925463
Tracking number: nfp0003

U.S. publication © 2010 New Forest Press
Published in arrangement with Black Rabbit Books

PO Box 784, Mankato, MN 56002
www.newforestpress.com

Printed in the USA
9 8 7 6 5 4 3 2 1

Every effort has been made to trace the copyright holders, and we apologize in advance for any omissions.
We would be pleased to insert the appropriate acknowledgments in any subsequent edition of this publication.

CONTENTS

Greenland

NORTH
AMERICA

Atlantic
Ocean

N

SOUTH
AMERICA

KEY
Ferdinand Magellan (1519–1522)
Francisco Pizarro (1530–1533)

THE VOYAGES OF MAGELLAN & PIZARRO

Russia

EUROPE

China

India

AFRICA

Indian
Ocean

Australia

FERDINAND MAGELLAN

When Christopher Columbus sailed across the Atlantic Ocean in 1492 his intention was to discover a westward route to China and the East Indies. An eastward route was blocked to Europeans by hostile Muslim lands. Columbus never found Asia, but he did discover, after four voyages, a continent virtually unknown to Europeans —America. However, Columbus and others continued to believe that it was possible to journey westward and reach Asia by sailing around the American continent. It was this dream that inspired Ferdinand Magellan to sail away on a quest that would become the first voyage to circumnavigate the world. Magellan proved that it was possible to reach Asia by traveling to the west, but he paid for this discovery with his life, as he was killed before the voyage was completed.

A WOODCUT PRINT OF MAGELLAN

Magellan was born in 1480 into a noble family in the Portuguese town of Sabrosa. He spent his early years as a page at the Portuguese royal court in Lisbon, before joining the Portuguese navy.

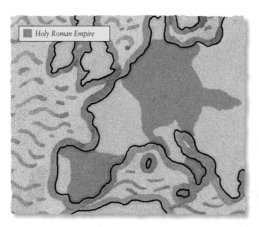

THE MOST POWERFUL MONARCH IN EUROPE

Charles V ruled over Spain, the Netherlands, southern Italy, most of modern-day Germany and Austria, and Spanish-conquered America and Africa, known as the "Holy Roman Empire." He provided the finance for Magellan's trip and continued to pay for the conquest and colonization of South and Central America.

THE TREATY OF TORDESILLAS

To prevent further rivalry between Spain and Portugal Pope Alexander VI issued the Treaty of Tordesillas in 1494. This gave Spain control over all non-Christian lands west of an imaginary line in the mid-Atlantic. Portugal was given everything to the east.

THE RISE OF PORTUGAL

This engraving of Lisbon in the 1550s shows that Portugal was an important and wealthy seafaring and trading nation. Portugal had successfully freed itself from Muslim rule by 1250 and turned its attention to the exploration of the Atlantic coast of West Africa. The Portuguese discovery of a route around Africa to Asia meant that they controlled the spice trade to Europe. It was for this reason that Spain financed Magellan's trip to find an alternative route to the East.

MAGELLAN TAKES TO THE SEA

While Magellan served with the Portuguese navy, he traveled to many parts of the world, including India and West Africa. He took part in battles against the Arabs on the Indian Ocean. Afterward, he fought against the Moors in North Africa, where he was injured. He asked the king of Portugal, Manuel I, for an increase in his pension. Manuel's response was to dismiss him and Magellan offered his services to Charles V.

FERDINAND MAGELLAN
-A TIMELINE-

~1476~
Francisco Pizarro born

~1480~
Ferdinand Magellan born

~1485~
Hernando Cortés born

~1494~
Treaty of Tordesillas between Spain and Portugal signed, dividing the non-Christian world between them

~1500~
Brazil discovered by Pedro Alvarez Cabral

~1502~
Pizarro sails for Hispaniola

Montezuma ascends the throne of the Aztec Empire

~1504~
Cortés sails for Hispaniola

KING JOHN II OF PORTUGAL

John II ruled Portugal from 1481 to 1495. He had been placed in charge of Portuguese explorations by his father, in 1474, and he encouraged the exploration of the African coast and the Middle East. Columbus had asked him for money to finance his trip across the Atlantic Ocean but John turned him down. In 1492, he admitted thousands of wealthy Jews into Portugal after they had been expelled by Spain, only to expel them a few years later in 1497–1498.

Preparing for the Voyage

MAGELLAN'S SHIPS

Of the five ships in Magellan's fleet, four, including the *Victoria (above)*, were carracks. Carracks were large vessels that were originally built to be merchant ships. On expeditions, they carried supplies and most of the weapons. The Santiago was a caravel. Caravels were much smaller and lighter, with triangular sails that made them better for navigating in coastal waters. Carracks had three masts or more, while the typical caravel only had two.

discover a westward route to Asia from the west. Charles I allowed Magellan to be commander of the fleet and to keep 5 percent of any profit made from the trip. Magellan took a close interest in how his ships were equipped, and records still exist that show exactly what Magellan took on his voyage. These include details of weapons, navigational instruments, food, and goods for trade. He had five ships; the *San Antonio*, the *Trinidad*, the *Concepción*, the *Santiago*, and the *Victoria*. The crews totaled more than 230 and were of many different nationalities, including French, Portuguese, Italian, African, and Malaysian. Magellan was the only non-Spanish officer.

THE SUPPORT OF THE KING

Charles I approved Magellan's plan and agreed to pay for the voyage in September 1518. It took Magellan one year to gather a crew and to prepare his ships at the Spanish port of Sanlúcar in Seville. It is likely that Magellan had no intention of sailing around the world and was planning to return by the same route that he was to take from Spain.

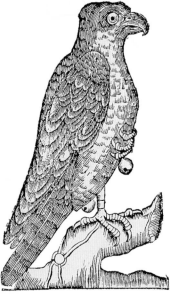

A HUNTING FALCON

Magellan knew that if his trip were to be successful, he had to trade with people that he met on his voyage. He took many things to barter with, such as printed handkerchiefs, scissors, knives, glass beads, and around 20,000 bells that could be attached to the feet of trained hunting birds. European explorers had found that many people in both America and Africa found hawkbells fascinating.

THE QUADRANT

Along with astrolabes, Magellan took 21 quadrants, which measured the angle between the horizon and the Sun or stars and gave the user his latitude position. Magellan also took a set of tables that showed the position of the Sun at different latitudes to enable him to calculate his position more accurately.

THE ASTROLABE

Magellan took seven astrolabes on his voyage. Astrolabes could find the latitude of a ship by measuring the height of the North Star or the noon Sun. This picture is of a land-based astrolabe, though the principles are the same for both.

MORE ON THE ASTROLABE

This is an Arabic example of an astrolabe. The instrument was considerably developed in the medieval Islamic world, where Arab astronomers introduced angular scales to it, adding circles indicating azimuths on the horizon. It was widely used throughout the Muslim world, chiefly as an aid to navigation and as a way of finding the Qibla, the direction of Mecca.

FERDINAND MAGELLAN
- A TIMELINE -

~1505~
Magellan joins the Portuguese navy

~1506~
Magellan sails to the East Indies

~1511~
Cuba conquered by Diego de Velazquez de Cuélla

~1513~
Magellan is injured while fighting in North Africa

Vasco Nunez de Balboa is the first European to see the Pacific Ocean

Juan Ponce de Leon discovers Florida

~1514~
The colony of Panama established

~1518~
After a quarrel with King Manuel I of Portugal, Magellan begins to work for Charles I of Spain. Charles V agrees to fund Magellan's voyage to find Asia

SHIPS & SAILING

The crews of the early voyages of exploration faced many dangers. Not only did they have to put up with cramped conditions and only a small supply of food and water (which was often bad), but they were sailing into the unknown with little idea where they were and how fast they were traveling. Perhaps it is not surprising, therefore, that the explorers often had to face mutiny. Today, ships have little trouble locating their exact position. Accurate maps, clocks, and global positioning satellites (GPS) mean that sailors can tell where they are to within a few feet. Sailors in the 1400s and 1500s were not so fortunate.

GETTING YOUR BEARINGS

The ancient Chinese discovered that lodestone is naturally magnetic and if suspended on a string will always point to the north. Early navigators made good use of this natural material but it was somewhat crude. Sometime in the 1100s, European navigators discovered that a needle could be similarly magnetised by stroking it with a lodestone. This discovery eventually led to the development of more sophisticated and accurate compasses, with the needle balanced on a central pivot. The example shown above is encased in an ivory bowl and dates from about 1580.

DEAD RECKONING

If a navigator knew where his ship sailed from, what its speed was, the direction the ship was traveling in, and how long they had been traveling, then it was possible to calculate how far they had traveled by "dead-reckoning" and so find their position. However, winds and tides meant that this was only an approximate way of figuring out the ship's position.

WEAPONS ON BOARD

Magellan knew that the voyage he was about to take was vulnerable to attack. He prepared for this by taking a large amount of weapons, including 1,000 lances, 60 crossbows, and 120 spears. He also had cannon similar to these, although cannon on board ships did not have wheels at this time.

THE CROSS-STAFF

The simplest way to measure the latitude of a ship was to use an instrument called a cross-staff. It had a crossbar for sighting and a rod with measurements cut into the side. The crossbar would be lined up between the Sun or North Star and the horizon. The measurements of the long piece of wood would then tell the navigator the angle of the Sun or star from the horizon. From this, he could figure out his latitude. There is considerable danger in staring at the sun for too long. In 1595, Captain John Davis invented the back-staff, which used mirrors and shadows so that navigators did not risk being injured.

TELLING THE TIME

For the navigator to calculate a ship's position, it was vital that he knew what time of day it was. Sailors would be given the job of watching a large sand-filled hourglass (similar to this 17th-century example, shown here). It normally emptied after 30 minutes and then a bell would be rung so that everybody on board knew what the time was.

NAVIGATION

In these days of radar, computer technology, and satellites, it is easy to underestimate the great navigational skills of the Elizabethan seafarers. For the large part they were sailing uncharted seas and had to estimate their position as best they could, using only the positions of heavenly bodies to guide them. Until the development of more refined instruments, such as the chronometer in the 1700s, navigation was a very inexact science and relied heavily on the observational skills of the individual. Needless to say, there were many accidents, particularly if the ships were blown off-course by bad weather into unknown waters.

GUIDED BY THE STARS

During the 1500s the cross-staff became commonly used to calculate a ship's latitude (north-south position) at night. It comprised two pieces of wood, similar in appearance to a crossbow, with graduated scales marked along the length. By observing the angle between the horizon and the North (or Pole) Star and taking a reading off the scale, coupled with a compass reading, the ship's approximate position could be calculated. Shown here is a buckstaff, invented about 1594, for measuring the height of the sun for the same purpose.

THE "MARINER'S MIRROUR"

Following Magellan's, and later Drake's, circumnavigation of the world, it became possible more accurately to assess the Earth's size, which led in turn to the production of more accurate charts. The first sea atlas to be published in England, in 1588, was the *Mariner's Mirrour*. It was a collection of maps and charts showing the known coastlines of the world, derived from Dutch originals. The Dutch were at that time an English ally against Spain and at the forefront of navigational techniques.

LODESTONE

One of the main problems facing navigators in the 1500s was accurately calculating a ship's longitude (east-west position). Here, the astronomer-mathematician Flavius tries to do so by floating a piece of lodestone (a form of iron oxide) in a bowl of water, whilst making calculations.

STEERING BY THE SUN

This view shows a 16th century navigator trying to calculate the ship's latitude by use of a compass and an early form of quadrant to measure the angle of the sun's rays. However, precise time-keeping was necessary to ensure the accuracy of the calculations so at best a ship's position could only be approximated. The first fully successful sea-clock (chronometer) was not developed until 1759.

ASTRONOMICAL INSTRUMENTS

By the 1500s, compasses and other astronomical instruments had become quite sophisticated, as can be seen in this beautifully crafted astronomical compendium. It was made of brass in 1569 by Humphrey Cole, one of the finest scientific instrument makers of the time, and was once believed to have belonged to Drake. The compendium comprised a compass, along with lunar and solar dials which, as well as being an astronomical aid, enabled the user to calculate the time. Engraved on the casing were the latitudes of many important ports around the world.

NAVIGATION -A TIMELINE-

~1588~

The first sea atlas, the "Mariner's Mirrour" is published in England

~1594~

The buckstaff is invented. It measures the height of the sun

~1759~

The first successful sea chronometer is produced

MAGNETIC COMPASS

It was vitally important that the sailors crossing the Atlantic Ocean knew exactly what direction they were sailing in. On a clear day or night, either the Sun or the North Star were used. They could also use a magnetic compass. The magnetic field around Earth meant that a magnetized needle floating in water would always point northward.

JACK-OF-ALL-TRADES

A crew on a 16th century ship had to be completely self-sufficient, for they were often away at sea for several years and might go many months between landings. As well as being able to handle the ship, sailors had to master other essential skills, such as carpentry, sailmaking, ropemaking, and cooking.

DRUNKENNESS

One of the common problems facing any captain commanding an early explorer's ship on a long voyage was boredom and the unruly behavior of his crew. With fresh water in short supply, the only drink available was beer (a gallon per crew member per day) or other stronger alcohols, which frequently led to drunkenness, not only on board but in port. Discipline was therefore very harsh to avoid potentially fatal accidents at sea.

LIFE ON BOARD

Life on board ship in the 1500s was extremely harsh and the pay (which was frequently in arrears) was very poor. But, faced with abject poverty on land at a time when many country people were being forcibly ejected from their land because of changing farming practices, many had little option. A fair proportion of a ship's crew would also have been criminals escaping justice, which often led to problems with discipline. The mortality rate amongst an average crew was very high and it would be considered normal for a ship to return to port with only a quarter of the men left alive. To ensure they had enough men left to make the return journey most captains oversubscribed when signing on a new crew, but this in itself led to problems of overcrowding and food rationing. Conditions on board were cramped, each man usually sleeping in a hammock slung below decks at his place of work. Toilet facilities were virtually non-existent.

DISEASE

The most common form of disease encountered aboard ship was scurvy, a deficiency of vitamin C, caused by lack of fresh fruit and vegetables. The symptoms include bleeding into the skin and teeth loosening. Resistance to infection is also lowered, often resulting in death if untreated. All ships carried their share of rats, which might spread infectious diseases such as plague. Other common diseases were malaria, typhoid, and dysentery.

THE ART OF THE GUNNER

Most 16th century ships carried a number of cannon (a mortar is shown here), usually made from cast iron or bronze. They were mounted on carriages and secured in place by heavy ropes to control the recoil when being fired and to prevent them coming adrift in heavy seas. They were used mostly to disable a ship before boarding.

THE CHATHAM CHEST

After the Armada of 1588, so many seamen were wounded and maimed that Sir John Hawkins established the "Chatham Chest"—the first seamen's charity. All sailors in the Navy had to pay six pence a month from their wages into it for welfare purposes. This is the chest of 1625.

HEALTH & SAFETY

The health and safety of the crew aboard a typical 16th century ship was, to say the least, extremely hazardous. There were many accidents in simply carrying out the day-to-day tasks of sailing. Injuries sustained during encounters with enemy vessels, usually at close quarters, were horrific. Most ships carried a surgeon, but the treatment he was able to administer was both limited and very crude. By far the most common form of treatment was the amputation of badly damaged or infected limbs. There was no anesthetic (other than to make the patient drunk) and the survival rate was appallingly low. Many of those who survived surgery died from gangrene afterward.

DAILY SUSTENANCE

All of the ship's food was prepared in the galley and then distributed among the crew. Food was rarely fresh and might consist of biscuit, salted beef, or fish, supplemented by cheese and gruel, a kind of porridge mix. Drinking water was usually scarce but most ships carried a plentiful supply of beer. The pieces of tableware shown here were retrieved from Henry VIII's ship the *Mary Rose* and are typical of items in use throughout the Tudor period.

LANDING AT RIO DE JANEIRO

Three months after setting sail from Spain, Magellan reached the Brazilian coast on December 6, 1519. Magellan was nervous because the entire area was controlled by Portugal. He sailed south until he landed at present-day Rio de Janeiro. After stocking up with fresh supplies, the ships continued south and spent that winter in San Julián in Patagonia.

THE SPANISH CAPTAINS MUTINY

After spending the winter in San Julián, Magellan invited all the captains to eat with him. None of them came, and instead they sent a demand that the fleet return to Spain. Magellan acted ruthlessly. The captain of the *Victoria* was killed, and others were either imprisoned or abandoned on the shore. In October 1520, as they neared the South Pole, the captain and crew of the *San Antonio* mutinied again and sailed back toward Spain.

AROUND THE TIP OF SOUTH AMERICA

On October 21, 1520, the ships entered what is today known as the Magellan Strait, although Magellan himself called it *Canal de Todos los Santos* (All Saints' Channel). The strait was a narrow and dangerous channel, and they were sailing straight into the wind. Sometimes the wind was so strong that the ships had to be towed by rowboats. It took them 38 days to sail through the strait. With only three ships left, Magellan eventually reached the Pacific Ocean on November 28, 1520.

SIGHTING STRANGE ANIMALS

Magellan and his men had sailed farther south than any other European, and they saw many different creatures. They caught animals such as seals and penguins for food. Pigafetta called the seals "sea wolves," and he thought that the penguins were geese. In his diary, he said "These geese are black . . . and they do not fly, and live upon fish. They have beaks like that of a crow."

SETTING OFF

The five ships sailed from Sanlúcar on September 20, 1519, with the *Trinidad* leading the way. An Italian nobleman, Antonio Pigafetta, kept diaries for the entire journey. From these diaries, it is clear that Magellan faced many difficulties on board the ship. The other officers on the voyage disliked Magellan because he was Portuguese, and they plotted against him. He had to deal with several mutinies during his voyage. At first, he had to treat the crew with care. Pigafetta says that he did not tell them where they were going "so that his men should not from amazement and fear be unwilling to accompany him on so long a voyage." After stopping for supplies at the Canary Islands, Magellan sailed along the West African coast in order to avoid Portuguese patrol ships before setting off across the Atlantic Ocean.

SAINT ELMO'S FIRE

The ships hit a massive Atlantic storm. The electrical charge created huge sparks that made the ships' masts appear to be on fire. The crew thought that the lights were saints protecting them and called them Saint Elmo's Fire.

SEARCHING FOR THE STRAIT

While sailing along the South American coast, Magellan sent ships ahead to search for the route around South America. He explored the entrance to the River Plate, thinking that it might be the entrance to the Pacific Ocean. The *Santiago* was sunk while searching for the strait, causing even more resentment among his crew.

THE VOYAGE COMPLETED

Magellan reached the Pacific Ocean more than one year after leaving Spain. He had put down two mutinies, lost one ship to a rebellious crew, and had another wrecked. When the three remaining ships left the strait, they became the first Europeans to sail into the Pacific Ocean. But, they were not the first Europeans to see the Pacific Ocean; Vasco de Balboa had this honor, he crossed Central America to the west coast by foot in 1513. Balboa had simply named the ocean the "Great South Sea." Magellan named it the Pacific Ocean because of the gentle winds that he found there. Many of his crew wanted to return home, but Magellan believed that it was now only a short journey to Asia. They sailed for three more months, seeing only two uninhabited islands (which they named the Unfortunate Islands), before finally landing in Guam.

THE HUGE OCEAN

The three-month journey across the ocean took its toll on the crew. Their biscuits had either been eaten by rats or were rotten. The water was too foul for many to drink. The crew was so desperate that they ate sawdust, rats, and strips of leather. Many became very sick with scurvy, and 29 died.

THE DEATH OF MAGELLAN

Cilapulapu, one of the islands of the Philippines, refused to accept Spanish rule. On April 27, 1521, Magellan and 60 armed men tried to subdue Cilapulapu. In the battle that followed, Magellan was hit by a spear and was then hacked to death.

ARRIVAL IN THE PHILIPPINES

It took another week for the fleet to sail from Guam and arrive at the Philippines. There, sick sailors were put ashore to recover and Magellan began trading with the local inhabitants. In exchange for some of the hawkbells and mirrors Magellan had brought with him, he was given a basket of ginger and a bar of gold.

MONUMENT TO MAGELLAN AT CEBU

When Magellan reached the island of Cebu after leaving the Philippines, he calculated that he was now west of the Spice Islands, which had already been visited by Europeans by traveling eastward. It was at this point that he knew it was possible to sail around the world.

LANDING AT GUAM

On March 6, 1521, Magellan reached the island of Guam, part of the modern-day Marianas Islands. There was obvious relief at reaching land and the opportunity to stock up with fresh supplies. The local people *(see left)* tried to steal one of their landing boats. Magellan reacted by calling the islands Ladrones, or Thieves, Islands. He also burned down a village to set an example.

FERDINAND MAGELLAN
-A TIMELINE-

~1519~
Panama City founded

Magellan's ships sail away from Spain

Cortés and his army enters Tenochtitlan

~DECEMBER 6, 1519~
Magellan arrives at the South American coast and then sails on to Rio de Janiero

~1520~
Magellan reaches San Julian in Argentina and spends the winter there

Magellan deals with the mutiny by his Spanish captains

The Aztecs drive Cortés out of Tenochtitlan

TIERRA DEL FUEGO

Sailing through the Magellan Straits at night, they saw many fires from distant Native American camps. They then called the land Tierra del Fuego, the "Land of Fires." Once through, the ships remained close while sailing up the west coast of South America.

THE JOURNEY HOME

When Magellan was killed, the *Trinidad* and the *Victoria* headed back to Spain. Only the *Victoria* completed the journey home. The voyage had brought no profit to the Spanish king but Magellan had proved that a westward route to Asia did exist.

Hernando Cortés & the Aztecs

The Spanish conquered Cuba in 1511 under the command of Diego de Velazquez. From there, they set out in ships to search for gold on the Central American mainland. In 1517, Francisco de Cordoba sailed to Yucatan on the mainland where he met the Maya people, but they quickly drove him away. Another expedition one year later was more successful, and they brought back gold to Cuba. In 1519, Velazquez ordered Hernando Cortés, who had helped in the conquest of Cuba, to lead an expedition to explore the interior of Mexico. An argument between the two men led to Cortés abandoning Velazquez and setting off with his own private army. Little did Cortés realize that he would encounter a great Empire, one of the largest cities in the known world, and that with only a few hundred soldiers he would destroy both.

HERNANDO CORTÉS

Hernando Cortés was born in 1485 into a Spanish noble family. He studied for two years at the University of Salamanca. In 1504, he arrived in the New World and fought in the conquest of Cuba in 1511.

MARINA THE TRANSLATOR

Soon after he landed in Yucatan, Cortés was given slaves as a gift by the local people. One of these was a woman whom the Spaniards named Marina. Her knowledge of the area and her ability to speak both the local Maya language and Nahuatl, the Aztec language, made her invaluable to Cortés. However, he still needed a Spaniard who could speak Mayan in order to talk to the Aztecs.

MOUNT POPOCATEPETL

On their way to the Aztec capital, the Spaniards passed the volcano of Mount Popocatepetl. It was belching smoke. They had never seen a live volcano before, and Cortés sent some men up the mountain to see where the smoke was coming from. They were forced back by the hot ash.

FIRST MEETING

This picture *(above)* shows the first meeting between Montezuma, the Aztec ruler, and Cortés. When Cortés and his men reached the Aztec capital, Montezuma was there to welcome him. He stood under a canopy of feathers, gold, silver, and jewels, and he wore magnificent clothes, including shoes with golden soles. He received Cortés and his men with honor and allowed them to enter Tenochtitlan, the Aztec capital.

WERE THE SPANIARDS GODS?

Cortés had only 600 soldiers and could easily have been defeated by the Aztec soldiers before they reached the capital. But Montezuma held back. It was a special year in the Aztec calendar when Quetzalcoatl, one of their gods, might return to the Aztecs and destroy them. It was said this god would be tall with white skin, a beard, and long dark hair. Cortés closely matched this description. Montezuma had to decide whether the Spaniards were men or gods. He decided that Cortés was the god that he was told would return, and he prepared to welcome him.

THE AZTECS SEE THE SPANISH

Montezuma heard about the Spaniards and sent messengers to meet them and report back. The messengers' report showed that the Spaniards, and their horses, looked very strange to them. "They dress in metal and wear metal hats on their heads. Their deer carry them on their backs wherever they wish to go. These deer are as tall as the roof of a house."

THE GREAT TEMPLE

At the very center of Tenochtitlan was the Great Temple, a single pyramid with two shrines. One was dedicated to Huitzilopochtli, god of war, and the other to Tlaloc, the rain god. The cutaway shows that several temples had been built on this site and that the Aztecs simply built each new temple over the old one.

THE WALLED PRECINCT

This model shows the complex of buildings that was isolated from the rest of Tenochtitlan. Alongside the huge temples were houses for the priests and recreation areas.

INSIDE THE TEMPLE

At the center of the Great Temple was the oldest inner temple. It was there that human sacrifices often took place.

COATEPANTLI

The wall around the complex was called the Coatepantli. It is believed that the wall was around 10 ft. (3m) high and each side measured around 1,300 ft. (400m). There were probably four gates that led into the area.

TEMPLE OF QUETZALCOATL

This circular temple was dedicated to Quetzalcoatl, the god of knowledge. The conical roof could have been made of straw.

AZTEC PYRAMIDS

Aztecs built their temples at the top of very high pyramids. The temples were used for their religious ceremonies and sacrifices. The sacrifices would take place at the entrance, after which the blood and limbs of the victims were swept down the steps.

THE AZTEC EMPIRE

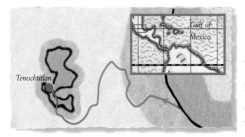

Cortés's journey to Tenochtitlan, 1519

When Cortés and his men arrived at Tenochtitlan, they had reached the center of a huge empire that stretched from the Atlantic to the Pacific coast. The Aztecs were a wandering tribe until they began to build the city of Tenochtitlan around a temple to one of their gods, Huitzilopochtli, around the year 1300. They built the city on a series of islands on Lake Texcoco. The city had aqueducts, canals, and a huge causeway linking it to the mainland. By the 1500s, it had a population of around 300,000 and was larger than any European city. The wealth of the Aztecs came from conquered peoples who had to pay tribute to them.

TLACHTLI

This was the first building seen after entering the west gate. It was used to play a ball game called Tlachtli. Played by ruling families, it involved hitting a rubber ball through a hoop with the shoulders or hips.

SACRIFICE

The Aztecs believed that their gods needed to be fed with blood if they were to survive. If the gods died, then the world would come to an end. Sacrificial victims were first stretched over a stone by four priests. The flint knife attached to this ornate hilt would have been used by a fifth priest to cut open the victim's chest for his still beating heart to be removed and placed in a bowl. The arms and legs of the victim were eaten. Most of the victims were prisoners captured in battles.

THE AZTEC EMPIRE

As the Spanish advanced through the Aztec Empire and entered Tenochtitlan, they encountered a civilization that must have seemed to them to be both very cruel and very advanced. The Aztecs had a huge and incredibly wealthy empire of at least 12 million people, advanced agriculture, a magnificent city with beautiful palaces, a zoo, and colorful gardens. They were the most powerful people in Central America. One of Cortés's soldiers, Bernal Diaz, later wrote of his encounter with the Aztecs "With such wonderful sights to gaze on, we did not know what to say, or if what we saw was real." Their calendars, ways of writing, and the gods that they worshiped may have sounded strange to the Spaniards, but Aztec life was as sophisticated as anything that would have been found in other parts of the known world.

A MULTITUDE OF GODS

The Aztecs believed in many gods and goddesses. Each one of them looked after an aspect of Aztec life. There were four important gods. Tlaloc was the god of rain and storms. Tezcatlipoca was the god of darkness and evil. Huitzilopochtli was the god of light and war. Quetzalcoatl was the god of life. The Aztec priests were very powerful people.

WRITING AND READING

The Aztecs did not use letters for writing words. Instead, they had a type of picture-writing system called glyphs (an example is shown left) in which every object was represented as a drawing. There were strict rules about how these drawings were created. Aztec books were called codices. They were made out of bark, and the pages were joined together to make one long book.

POLE CEREMONY

Aztec religion demanded many different ceremonies and rituals. In one of these, men would use feathers to dress themselves as birds and would then be attached to ropes and swung around in a wide circle. As the photograph shows, this practice is still continued in modern-day Mexico.

PLAYING PATOLLI

Along with ball games such as Tlachtli, the Aztecs also played board games like Patolli. The board was divided into four sections and made 52, symbolizing the 52 years of the Aztec century. The game involved throwing dice and different colored beans until one player had three beans in a row. This and other games were often of religious significance and would have dire consequences—the loser and his family could become slaves. In Tlachtli, players were often badly injured, and the loser might be sacrificed.

AZTEC CALENDAR STONE

This large stone, one of the largest Aztec sculptures found, shows their belief that the world has been through four stages that have been created and destroyed. The Aztecs believed that they were living in the fifth age, which would be destroyed by a massive earthquake. The human race and the Sun and the Moon were created at the start of the fifth world. At the center of the stone is the face of the Sun.

COAST NEAR CEMPOALLA

The Aztecs were wealthy because the people they conquered had to pay tribute to them. When the Aztecs took over new lands, they allowed the people living there to continue following their own lives as long as they sent a tribute every year. This tribute was usually locally produced food. On the coast of Cempoalla, this would have been fish.

THE DEATH OF MONTEZUMA

When Cortés first left the city, fighting had broken out between the Aztecs and the Spanish. The Aztec leaders decided to depose the imprisoned Montezuma and replace him with his brother Cuitlahuac. Cortés did not realize that Montezuma was no longer seen as the ruler of the Aztecs, and he brought him to the roof of the royal palace to appeal to his people, but they replied by throwing stones at him and attacking the palace. One of the stones hit Montezuma, and he was later found dead. Both sides accused the other of killing him. His body was taken away and thrown into one of the nearby canals.

THE SIEGE BEGINS

Along with his new army, Cortés also had built 12 or 13 ships, which he armed with cannon from Cuba. These he used on the lake that surrounded the island city of Tenochtitlan to bombard the Aztec defenders. The Aztecs found themselves attacked from both inside and outside their city. Starving and weak with diseases, the Aztecs held out against the Spanish and their allies for several months.

FERDINAND MAGELLAN
-A TIMELINE-

~1520~

The strait between the Atlantic and Pacific oceans is sighted and, after several months, Magellan emerges into the Pacific

~1521~

Magellan lands at Guam/Ladrones Islands, followed by the Philippines, where he is killed

Fighting between Aztecs and Spaniards starts

Cortés returns to Tenochtitlan with a new army, and the Aztecs finally surrender

SMALLPOX IN THE CITY

In the end, it was not Spanish weapons that defeated the Aztecs. An outbreak of smallpox, a disease brought over from Europe, spread throughout the city, and many people died even before the siege began.

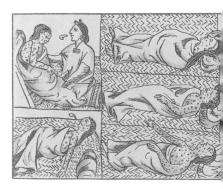

The Destruction of the Aztec Empire

After several days in Tenochtitlan, Cortés and his small army began to worry about their safety. They had seen the blood-stained steps of the Aztec temples and thought that the Aztecs were devil-worshipers. They felt that it was only Montezuma who stopped the Aztecs from killing them all. Cortés decided to take Montezuma prisoner and to use him to rule the Aztecs. By then, Montezuma must have realized that these men were not gods. Cortés stayed for several months before leaving to deal with a rival expedition from Cuba.

THE EMPIRE DESTROYED

Cuahtemoc, the nephew of Montezuma, became the new Aztec ruler and had to face Cortés's attack. He held out for four months, fighting on the streets of Tenochtitlan, before finally surrendering in August 1521. He was tortured and hanged.

AZTEC GOLD

The Aztecs believed that they could appease the Spanish by giving them huge amounts of gold. Montezuma took them to the treasure house where, according to one Aztec, "The Spaniards stripped the feathers from the golden shields. They put all the gold in one large pile and set fire to everything else, even if it was valuable. They then melted the gold and turned it into bars."

CORTÉS RETURNS

It was while Cortés was away that the Spaniards attacked the Aztecs. Cortés returned and tried to use Montezuma to calm the Aztecs, but the royal palace was besieged, and he had to fight his way out of Tenochtitlan. In May 1521, he came back with an army of 100,000 local people, who hated the Aztecs. He cut off all supplies of food and water to the city before launching his final attack.

THE INCA EMPIRE

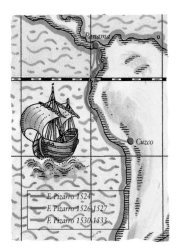

In what is now part of modern-day Peru, Ecuador, Argentina, Chile, and Bolivia rose the Andean empire of the Incas, which was even larger than the Aztec Empire. The empire expanded in the 1300s (from what is now Ayacucho in Peru) under the leadership of Pachacutec. According to accounts given to the Spanish, most of the Inca Empire was created under his rule. By the time the Incas came into conflict with the Spanish, they controlled a population of around 12 million people and stretched 2,480 mi. (4,000km) from south to north. This is remarkable given that the Incas did not possess horses or wheeled vehicles.

MODERN ANDEAN WOMAN

The legacy of the Incas still lives on. Even though the ancestors of the people of the Andean lands had been subjected to conquest, colonization, and Spanish rule, many aspects of Inca life are still in evidence today. The Incas would have recognized the way that these people still farm and fish. The clothes worn by this woman have changed little in style.

INCA GODS

Like the Aztecs, the Incas worshiped many gods. The most important god was Viracocha. He emerged from Lake Titicaca and then created the first men from clay. Under him were gods of the earth, the sea, storms, the Sun, the Moon, and the stars. Every season there were celebrations for different gods. Inti, the sun god, was particularly important, as the Inca rulers believed that they were descended from him. At Cuzco, there was a temple dedicated to Inti in which the doors were completely covered in gold.

THE CITY OF CUZCO

The city on the right of this picture was Cuzco, the capital city of the Incas. It was designed in the form of a puma, because the puma represented strength and power to the Incas. A fortress at one end was the head, and two rivers were straightened out to form the tail. The buildings were made of massive stone blocks that fit together so well that no mortar was needed to keep them together.

FERDINAND MAGELLAN
-A TIMELINE-

~1522~

Magellan's ship Victoria *arrives back in Spain*

~1523~

Guatemala conquered and settled by Pedro de Alvarado

~1524~

Cortés leads an expedition to Honduras

The colony of Nicaragua established

INCA TECHNOLOGY

These three pictures show how advanced Inca technology was. The picture on the far left shows the rope bridges that the Incas built to link their 12,400 mi. (20,000km) of paved roads. The center picture shows how they used lengths of string called quipos to keep count of things. The picture on the right shows some of the sophisticated methods used in their agriculture.

ATAHUALPA SEIZED

The Spaniards used the same methods to subdue the Incas as they used against the Aztecs. The Inca ruler, Atahualpa, had invited the Spaniards into his kingdom and met them at the town of Cajamarca. He was handed a *Bible*, which he threw away. The Spanish soldiers then captured him and attacked Atahualpa's followers.

ATAHUALPA AS A PRISONER

A Spaniard named Francisco de Xeres wrote a book about the conquest of the Incas in 1534. According to him, the Spanish commander, Francisco Pizarro, "presently ordered native clothes to be brought, and when Atabaliba was dressed, he made him sit near him and soothed his rage and agitation at finding himself so quickly fallen from his high estate."

THE INCA EMPIRE

One of the most spectacular monuments of the Inca empire is the ruined town of Machu Picchu. It lay undiscovered until it was found by an American archeologist, Hiram Bingham, in 1911. It was never discovered by the Spanish invaders, so they did not have the chance to destroy it. It might have been a frontier outpost and was probably dedicated to Inti, the sun god.

MACHU PICCHU

Machu Picchu is around 50 mi. (80km) northwest of Cuzco and is almost 7,900 ft. (2,400m) above sea level.

THE DESTRUCTION OF THE INCA EMPIRE

ATHABALIBA
ultimus Rex Peruanorum

The Spaniards in Central America heard rumors of a land in the south called Biru, or Peru, that was filled with gold and other precious metals. Francisco Pizarro decided to sail down the coast from the town of Panama, which the Spaniards had built in 1519. He led an expedition in 1527 and discovered the city of Tumbez. They were welcomed by the inhabitants and shown a lot of gold and silver. Pizarro was now convinced that he had found a huge source of gold, and he returned to Spain. Charles V gave him permission to conquer this new land and made him Governor and Captain-General of Peru. He returned in 1530 with an army of around 180 soldiers.

CIVIL WAR

Pizarro was certainly helped by the fact that the Incas were fighting a civil war. Inca rulers were called the Sapa Inca. In 1527, the Sapa Inca, Huayna Capac, died of smallpox. He had two sons, Huascar and Atahualpa, who both claimed his title. The final battle was fought as Pizarro approached and Huascar had been taken prisoner.

DEMAND FOR GOLD

After he was taken prisoner himself, Atahualpa thought that if he gave the Spaniards enough gold to fill a large room they would let him go. Pizarro agreed to release him and Atahualpa ordered gold to be stripped from temples and palaces. More than 7 metric tons of gold were collected and melted down.

FRANCISCO PIZARRO

Unlike many Spanish explorers, Pizarro was not born into a noble family. He was uneducated and could not read or write. He worked on a farm before coming to Central America to seek his fortune. He was killed during a power struggle in Lima in 1541.

THE END OF THE INCAS

With the death of Atahualpa, Inca resistance subsided. The Spaniards entered Cuzco on November 15, 1533. In 1536, Manco Inca, a puppet ruler, rose against the Spanish and nearly succeeded in driving them out. It took another 36 years to finally subdue the entire Inca Empire.

ATAHUALPA EXECUTED

Atahualpa had already been deceived once, and now Pizarro was ready to deceive him again, since he did not intend to release him. Pizarro wanted more than gold. He also planned to rule the Incas. On July 16, 1533 he had Atahualpa strangled with a piece of rope. He was baptized just before his death so that his soul was "saved." His sisters asked to be buried alive with him, but the shocked Spaniards, who attended the funeral, refused.

FERDINAND MAGELLAN
-A TIMELINE-

~1524~
Quito taken by Sebastian de Belalcazar

~1532~
Atahualpa seized by Pizarro

~1533~
Atahualpa executed, and Cuzco finally taken

Ecuador conquered by Sebastian de Belalcazar

PIZARRO AND ATAHUALPA MEET

Atahualpa was certainly confident after defeating his brother, and he was curious to meet Pizarro. Although he took 3,000 soldiers with him to the meeting, he agreed that they would be unarmed after Pizarro said that he would not be harmed. The Spanish soldiers, although they were vastly outnumbered, brought their muskets and cannon with them. When Atahualpa was captured, hundreds of his soldiers were killed trying to defend him with no weapons.

EUROPEAN DISEASES

One of the main reasons for the terrible drop in population was the introduction of diseases such as smallpox and measles into the American continent. The people of South and Central America had no resistance to these new diseases, and many died as a result.

BECOMING EUROPEAN

The Spanish and Portuguese conquerors felt that their way of life and religion were better than those of the people they had conquered. This picture shows that people were forced out of their native clothes and made to wear European fashions. It was hoped that this would make them more European.

SURVIVING CUSTOMS

The Europeans did not succeed in completely destroying the cultures they came across. This mask shows that modern Mexicans still celebrate the "Day of the Dead," which has its origins with the Aztecs. Even today many people in South and Central Americans add bits of their old religions to their Christian worship.

DESTROYING IDOLS

The priests who traveled with the explorers were determined that the conquered people would become Christian. Many of these people felt that they had been defeated by a superior god and readily converted. The priests also stamped out all signs of the old religions by pulling down the temples and smashing the statues of gods. They replaced them with crosses and statues of the Virgin Mary.

LIFE IN SPANISH AMERICA

The arrival of the Spanish and the Portuguese in South and Central America had a devastating effect upon the people who were living there. In only a few years huge empires were destroyed by small groups of determined and cruel men driven by greed, personal ambition, and religious zeal. These new rulers did not respect the ideas and customs of their new subjects. All over the conquered empires the Spaniards and Portuguese looted and destroyed. The population of Mexico was estimated to be 25 million in 1519. From disease and murder that figure had plummeted to nearly 2 million by 1580.

INDEPENDENCE

It was only in the first part of the 1800s that South and Central America finally broke away from their European rulers. It was the revolutionary Simon Bolivar who led many countries toward independence. Paraguay became independent in 1813, followed by Argentina in 1816. Chile followed in 1818 and then Mexico and Peru in 1821.

NEW BUILDINGS

Once the Spaniards had destroyed the temples and buildings they came across, they began to build on top of the ruins. Churches, such as this one in Cuzco, were built on the sites of old temples. Mexico City was built on the remains of Tenochtitlan, using the stones from the dismantled buildings.

HARSH PUNISHMENTS

As more and more people from Spain came over to Mexico and South America, conditions for the conquered people continued to get worse. Thousands were enslaved and made to work in gold and silver mines where they suffered from terrible conditions and from overwork. This meant that their fields were left untended, and many more went hungry. Anyone who disobeyed the Spanish was dealt with severely. This picture shows people being burned alive by their Spanish master.

THE IMPACT OF SOUTH AMERICA ON EUROPE

From the ruined palaces of ancient empires through to the magnificent churches built by the Spanish and Portuguese, it is clear even today that the arrival of Europeans on American shores had a huge and devastating impact. Although it is more difficult to see the influence that South and Central America had on the lives of Europeans, it nevertheless had a similar impact. The most obvious was the huge amount of gold and silver that was taken to Spain. The Spanish king claimed one fifth of all gold and silver that was mined. This made Spain one of the most powerful and wealthiest nations in Europe. It is still possible to see Spanish churches decorated with gold that came from their conquered lands. Much of the food that we now take for granted was first grown in these lands.

NUTS AND BEANS

Many vegetables, such as peanuts, sweet potatoes, and kidney beans, originally came from South and Central America. They are now grown all over the world. Peanuts *(above)* are native to South America. They were first introduced to Africa by European explorers and then reached North America with the slave trade. They are now cultivated all over the world from India to Nigeria and the United States. Sweet potatoes are native to Central America and were an important part of the Aztec diet and were also found in the Andes. They were taken to Europe in the 1500s and then later spread to Asia.

A Sᵗᵐ Prinsipal con su negra esclava
Arbol de Granadillas, y su Fruta.
Arbol del Mispero, y su Fruta
Fruta con nombre de Nar...
Palma de Cocos grandes
Arbol de Coquitos de el...

SQUASHES

Squashes such as pumpkins and zucchini were central to the diets of people in Central America. There is some evidence that they were beginning to be eaten by Native Americans in North America before the 1400s. However, it was the arrival of the Spanish explorers that speeded up the spread of squashes. They are now grown and eaten all over the world, particularly in Mediterranean countries and North America.

RUBBER AND MAHOGANY

Rubber was used by the peoples of America for centuries. Christopher Columbus observed the inhabitants of Haiti using rubber to make balls for games. The Aztecs used rubber balls to play Tlachtli. But it was not until the start of the 1800s, when a way was found of keeping rubber soft when it became solid, that it began to be used commercially. Mahogany has been used for making fine furniture since 1500. European demand for mahogany led to many South American forests being cleared. Their continued destruction is a major concern for modern environmentalists.

FERDINAND MAGELLAN
-A TIMELINE-

~1535~
Lima founded by Pizarro

~1537~
The Chibchas of Columbia are conquered by Gonzalo Jimenez de Quesada

~1540~
Cortés returns to Spain

~1541~
Pizarro assassinated

Mississippi discovered by Hernando de Soto

~1542~
Orellana reaches the mouth of the Amazon

~1547~
Cortés dies near Seville

MAIZE

Along with the sweet potato, maize was the most important crop of both South and Central America. The Aztecs ground maize into flour, which was then turned into tortillas or tamales which were stuffed with vegetables or atolli, a type of porridge. The Incas also used maize to make a porridge called capia. The United States now grows nearly half of all the world's maize.

OTHER EXPLORERS OF SOUTH AMERICA

Although the Spanish explorers had a reputation for being bloodthirsty and cruel, it must be remembered that they conquered the great civilizations of the Aztecs and Incas with only a few hundred soldiers. This must have taken a lot of courage, daring, and a certain amount of good luck. Pizarro and Cortés were not the only explorers of South and Central America. Many more men set out into unexplored areas with little idea of the dangers that lay ahead of them.

PEDRO DE ALVARADO

Alvarado was second in command to Cortés during the conquest of the Aztecs. After Tenochtitlan was destroyed and Mexico City built, he became its first mayor. In 1523, he conquered and settled Guatemala, and he later assisted in the conquest of Honduras.

JUAN PONCE DE LEON

De Leon was born in 1460 and sailed with Columbus in 1493. He spent most of his time either in Cuba or fighting in Puerto Rico. While he was in Cuba, he heard rumors of an island that had the fabled Fountain of Youth. He set sail to find the fountain, but instead he landed in Florida, his most famous discovery.

PEDRO ARIAS DAVILA

Davila established Spanish colonies in Panama in 1514 and Nicaragua in 1524. He also founded Panama City in 1519. It was Davila who first sent Pizarro to conquer the Incas. He became governor of Nicaragua in 1526, where he stayed until his death in 1531.

PEDRO ALVAREZ CABRAL

Cabral discovered Brazil almost by accident. In 1500, he had been sent by the king of Portugal to sail to India along the African coast. Soon after he set off, he was blown too far west and he reached land, which he named the Island of the True Cross. It was later called Brazil. He then set sail for India, but on the way he lost five of the 13 ships pictured here.

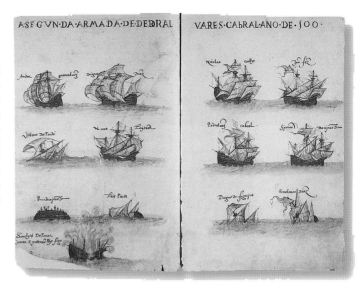

VASCO NUNEZ DE BALBOA

Balboa was an adventurer who stowed away on a ship from Hispaniola in the Caribbean to San Sebastian in Central America. He convinced the people there to resettle and then made himself their leader. He heard rumors of a huge sea and set off across Panama, with only a few hundred men, to find it. He was the first European to see the Pacific Ocean, which he claimed for Spain.

HERNANDO DE ALARCON

Alarcon commanded two ships that supported an overland expedition in 1540 from Mexico into the region now known as the southwestern United States. Alarcon sailed to the head of the Gulf of California and proved that there was no water passage between the Gulf and the Pacific Ocean. He was also one of the first Europeans to sail along the Colorado River.

SEBASTIAN DE BELALCAZAR

Belalcazar served under Pedro Arias Davila during his campaign in Nicaragua in 1524. He then joined Pizarro on his expedition to Peru in 1531. In 1533, he set out on his own and conquered the Incas in Ecuador.

PANFILO DE NARVÁEZ

Under the command of Diego Velazquez, Narváez played an important part in the conquest of Cuba in 1511. In 1520, he was sent to Mexico to arrest Cortés for treason. Cortés took him prisoner and released him one year later. In 1527, he led a two-year expedition to Florida. Narváez drowned, and only four of his men returned to Mexico.

ALVAR NUNEZ CABEZA DE VACA

De Vaca joined the expedition to Florida under the leadership of Panfilo de Narváez. The expedition was a disaster, and De Vaca was the only officer to survive. He and three other men eventually got back to Mexico. He was appointed the Governor of the South American province of Rio de la Plata—what is now modern-day Paraguay. In 1541, he led an expedition from Santos in Brazil to Asuncion in Paraguay, a journey of over 1,000 mi. (1,600km).

HERNANDO DE SOTO

De Soto is best known as the discoverer of the Mississippi River. He fought with Pizarro in the conquest of the Incas and was the first European to meet the Inca ruler, Atahualpa. With the backing of the Spanish king, he led an expedition to Florida in 1539. He traveled through Florida, North and South Carolina, Alabama and Mississippi. He discovered the Mississippi River in 1541.

OTHER EXPLORERS OF SOUTH AMERICA

Explorers went to America for many reasons. The stories of the incredible wealth of South and Central America that found their way back to Spain must have persuaded many to try to make their fortunes in these newly discovered lands. This is one of the reasons why the Spaniards treated their new subjects with such cruelty. Although the Spanish king and some priests tried to protect the people from being badly treated, they had little effect. Many of these explorers were interested only in getting rich as quickly as possible and they were not concerned about those that they had conquered. However, there were some who were driven by the belief that they were working for the glory of their god and country.

FRANCISCO DE ORELLANA

Orellana was the first person to explore the River Amazon. During an expedition into the interior of South America, Orellana found the Amazon and sailed along it for eight months until he reached the Atlantic Ocean. He then continued to Spain.

GONZALO JIMENEZ DE QUESADA

De Quesada was the Spanish conqueror of the Chibcha civilization of Columbia. In 1536, he set off to search for the legendary city of El Dorado. In 1537, he conquered the Chibchas and called the territory New Granada. While there, he founded the town of Bogota.

BERNAL DIAZ DEL CASTILLO

Del Castillo was a Spanish soldier who kept a record of the conquest of the Aztecs by Cortés. Before joining Cortés, he had visited Panama and went to Yucatan in 1517 and 1518. In 1519, he accompanied Cortés to Mexico and claimed to have fought in more than 100 battles. He also fought in the conquest of El Salvador and Guatemala.

DID YOU KNOW?

What ships the Europeans used as trading vessels?
In the first part of the 1500s the carrack became the most popular European ship for trade, exploration, and warfare. Carracks became important symbols of national pride. In England, Henry VIII had built the *Great Harry*, which was the largest carrack built up until that time. The French responded by building *La Grande Françoise*, which was even larger. Sadly, it was so large that it could not get out of the mouth of the harbor where it was built. By the end of the 1500s, the carrack was being replaced by the galleon.

What the biggest problem faced by sailors was?
The main problem faced by sailors on long voyages was scurvy. This often fatal disease is caused by a lack of vitamin C, which comes from fresh fruit and vegetables. Fresh food did not last long on the ships of the explorers. Sailors would become extremely tired and would start to bleed from the scalp and the gums. However, it was not until 1915 that vitamins were identified. Citrus fruit juice (ascorbic acid) was adopted against scurvy by the Admiralty in 1795 but before that fresh air, dry clothing, warmth, and exercise were also thought to help prevent it. There was thus much confusion about its exact cause.

Where the term "a square meal" comes from?
It is not known when this term first came into use but since at least Tudor times meals on board ship were dished up on square platters, which seamen balanced on their laps. They had frames around the edge to prevent the food from falling off and were so shaped to enable them to be easily stored when not in use. Each sailor thus received his full ration, or square meal, for the day.

How the Spice Islands got their name?
One of the main attractions for the 16th century explorers searching for new trade routes were spices from the East. The groups of islands that make up the East Indies (which include the Moluccas, Philippines, and Melanesia groups of islands) were particularly rich in such commodities and came to be known collectively as the Spice Islands.

How time gives longitude?
Each day (24 hours) Earth turns through 360°, from west to east; that is, it turns through 15° of longitude every hour and 1° every 4 minutes. A place that has a 4-minute difference in time at noon from a starting point (or prime meridian) to east or west—noon in each spot being when the Sun is exactly overhead—is 1° of longitude away. Thus, accurate east/west time variations between places can be converted into relative distances and positions of longitude.

We still use the stars for navigation?
It is easy to assume that because navigational techniques used in the past were relatively simple they were also inaccurate. This is not necessarily true, although results need to be accurately recorded and verified to be usable. In 1967 astronomers discovered pulsars, rapidly rotating condensed stars (formed from dead stars) that emit radio waves, or pulses, as detectable beams. They pulsate at fixed rates making it possible for future space programs to utilize them for navigational purposes in outer space.

How much European explorers were involved in slavery?
From the 1440s the Portuguese used their expeditions along the West African coast to capture people and to take them back to Portugal to sell as slaves. Europeans felt that slavery was justified because the people they had captured were not Christians. Once they became slaves then they could become Christians. Africans began to fight back once they realized why the Europeans were there. Portuguese traders soon realized that it would be easier to buy slaves from traders in the Benin.

How the Portuguese discovered Brazil?
When Vasco da Gama returned to Portugal from the Indies, Pedro Cabral set off from Lisbon with a fleet of 13 ships in March 1500. Like da Gama, he began by sailing westward. However, he went much further than he intended. On April 22, he sighted the coast of Brazil. After claiming the land for Portugal he set off eastward for the Indies.

For instance, 4 Dog was a good day to be born on. Anybody born on 2 Rabbit would not do so well. 1 Ocelot was seen as a good day for traveling.

That of all the continents, Antarctica is the coldest, driest, highest, and windiest?

Antarctica covers an area half as large again as the U.S. A. (about 5.5 million sq. mi./14 million sq. km.) and represents a tenth of the Earth's land mass. Approximately 98 percent of Antarctica is covered by ice, up to 1.5 mi. (2.4km) thick in places. The Elizabethan explorers had searched in vain for a habitable land mass in the southern oceans, which was not finally discovered until 1820, when Edward Bransfield landed on part of the Antarctic Peninsula.

What the history of the ancient civilizations was before the explorers "discovered" them?

We know very little about the lives of the Aztecs and Incas because the Spaniards destroyed everything that they found. Beautiful gold objects were melted down into gold bars. Books and drawings were burnt as works of the devil. Bishop Diego de Landa Calderón of Yucatán came across come painted books and he wrote later: "We found a great number of books in these letters of theirs, and because they had nothing but superstition and lies of the devil, we burned them all, which upset the Indians greatly, and caused them much pain." Most of the remains of Tenochtitlan were not discovered until the Mexicans began to build an underground railway system in Mexico City.

How America got its name?

America was named after the 16th-century navigator and mapmaker Amerigo Vespucci. Of Italian birth, in 1508 he was created Chief Royal Pilot of Spain. All Spanish captains had to provide him with full details each time they undertook a new voyage so that he could constantly amend and update his collection of sea charts. He made several voyages to the New World himself (notably in 1499–1500) and was once credited with discovering America. Although this was not true, he was the first to consider it to be an independent continent and not part of Asia. It was afterwards known as "Amerigo's Land" in honor of him.

How the Aztec calendar worked?

The Aztec calendar stone worked in a very peculiar way. The calendar was made up of two wheels, one of top of the other. The small wheel had 13 numbers carved or painted on it. The large wheel had the names of 20 days on it. These were the names of animals or plants. Numbers could then be lined up with a particular named day. Only the Aztec priests could read these and tell if a day was to be lucky or unlucky.

GLOSSARY

administer To give or dispense.

ally A person, group, or country that has joined with another for a particular purpose.

amputation The surgical removal of a limb or body part.

anesthetic A drug that causes temporary loss of sensation in the body.

aqueduct A channel or pipe built to carry water over a long distance.

armada A large fleet of warships.

arrears An unpaid debt that is overdue.

assassination To murder for pay or political reasons.

astronomical Relating to the study of the universe beyond Earth.

baptism A Christian ceremony that signifies spiritual cleansing and rebirth.

bombardment The heavy, continuous attacking of a target with artillery.

canopy A covering made of cloth hung or held up over something.

caravel A small, fast Spanish or Portuguese ship from the 1400s–1600s.

carpentry The occupation of making or repairing things in wood.

carrack A large merchant ship from the 1300s–1600s.

causeway A raised road or path across water or land that is wet.

chronometer An instrument for measuring time.

circumnavigate To travel all the way around something by ship.

civil war A war between different groups in the same country.

colonization The extension of a nation's power by the establishment of settlements and trade in foreign lands.

commission A committee set up to deal with and look at a certain issue.

compendium A collection of things.

conical Having the shape of a cone.

conquer To get or overcome by force.

crossbow A bow on a wooden support.

dead reckoning A way of estimating one's current position based on a known previous position, allowing for speed, distance, and direction moved.

deck A platform built on a ship. There are often numerous decks within a ship.

dedicate To devote to a particular person.

dysentery An inflammatory infection of the intestines resulting in severe diarrhea. Dysentery was a major cause of death on board ship.

electrical charge Electrical energy that has been stored.

engrave To cut a design or lettering into.

equator The imaginary line running around the center of Earth from east to west, at an equal distant from the North and South Poles.

expulsion The act of forcing something or someone out.

finance To provide money for.

fleet A group of navy ships under one command.

flint A hard gray rock.

gangrene The decomposition of body tissue caused by an infection.

GPS Satellite system that allows users to pinpoint their location.

hawkbells Bells attached to the legs of a hawk by a small leather strap, just above the talons. Bells were often organized to ring with different tones, so that in a group of hawks a pleasant sound would be produced. Hawking was a popular country sport where the hawk hunted for its owner.

hilt The handle of a sword or knife.

horizon The line where earth and the sky appear to meet.

hostile Feeling or showing dislike.

inhabitants Someone or something that lives in a place.

interior The inland part of a country.

kingdom A country with a king or queen at its head.

lance A weapon with a long pole and pointed metal.

latitude The imaginary parallel lines running east to west around Earth.

longitude The imaginary parallel lines running north to south around Earth.

malaria A disease spread by the bite of a mosquito.

mast A long upright pole that rises from the bottom of a sailboat or ship to support the sails and lines.

merchant ships A ship used for trade.

mortality The likelihood of death. The mortality rate is the rate of death in a certain number of people in a population.

musket A muzzle-loading smoothbore gun (without rotational grooves to guide the projectile along the barrel) mounted in and fired from the shoulder.

mutiny A rebellion by members of a ship's crew to overthrow the captain.

native A person born in a particular place or country, and living there.

page A young person who worked as a servant for a person such as a king.

pension Money paid at regular times by a former employer to a person who has retired, or by the government to a person who is not able to work.

puma A large wild cat with tan or gray fur and no spots.

puppet ruler A leader who is under the control of an outside force or influence.

pyramid A building or structure with triangular sides, narrowing to a peak at the top.

sacrifice The gift of something to a god as an act of worship.

siege A military act of surrounding a city or base, attacking it, and cutting off supplies.

smallpox A contagious disease which causes fever and pus-filled pimples.

spear A weapon with a long wooden shaft and a sharp pointed tip.

strait A narrow sea-channel, joining two larger bodies of water.

subdue To put down or contain by force or by authority.

surgeon A medical doctor who does surgery.

surgery The field of medicine that treats disease and injury by fixing or removing parts of the body.

sustenance Food and drink regarded as a source of strength; nourishment.

tribute The tax system employed by the Aztecs to support their state. This was paid by all the regions under their control to finance building, military, nobility, and religion.

Tudor Of or relating to the English royal family that held the throne from the accession of Henry VII in 1485 until the death of Elizabeth I in 1603.

typhoid An illness caused by eating or drinking contaminated food or water.

wealth A large amount of money or property.

FURTHER READING
& WEBSITES

BOOKS

Atlas of Exploration
Andrew Kerr and Francois Naude
(Dorling Kindersley Publications, 2008)

A Voyage You'd Rather Not Make
Mark Bergin (Children's Press (CT), 2006)

Explorer (Eyewitness)
Rupert Matthews (Dorling Kindersley, 2003)

Explorers: Atlas In The Round
Charlie Watson (Running Press Kids, 2001)

Explorers and Exploration
Steadwell Books and Lara Rice Bergen
(Heinemann Library, 2001)

*Explorers of the South Pacific: A Thousand Years of
Exploration, from the Polynesians to Captain Cook
and Beyond*
Daniel E. Harmon (Mason Crest Publishers, 2002)

Ferdinand Magellan: A Primary Source Biography
Lynn Hoogenboom (PowerKids Press, 2006)

*Ferdinand Magellan: Circumnavigating the World
(In the Footsteps of Explorers)*
Katharine Bailey (Crabtree Publishing Company, 2006)

*New York Public Library Amazing Explorers:
A Book of Answers for Kids*
Brendan January (Wiley, 2001)

Magellan: A Voyage Around the World (Expedition)
Fiona MacDonald (Franklin Watts, 1998)

Magellan's World (Great Explorers)
Stuart Waldman (Mikaya Press, 2007)

The Look-It-Up Book of Explorers (Look-It-Up Books)
Elizabeth Cody Kimmel (Random House, 2004)

*The World Made New: Why the Age of Exploration
Happened and How It Changed the World*
Marc Aronson (National Geographic, 2007)

*Tools of Navigation: A Kid's Guide to the History and
Science of Finding Your Way (Tools of Discovery)*
Rachel Dickinson (Nomad Press, 2005)

Who Was Ferdinand Magellan?
S. A. Kramer (Grosset & Dunlap, 2004)

You Are the Explorer
Nathan Aaseng (Oliver Press, 1999)

WEBSITES

*http://academickids.com/encyclopedia/index.php/
Ferdinand_Magellan*
An encyclopedic biography of Magellan with great
cross-referencing to subjects related to his voyages.

*www.kidskonnect.com/subject-index/16-history/
265-explorers.html*
A gateway to sites about the different explorers.

*www.lancsngfl.ac.uk/curriculum/history/index.php?
category_id=22*
An interactive introduction to the topic of
16th century exploration, from the Lancashire Grid
for Learning, England.

www.mariner.org/education/age-exploration
Useful information from the Mariners' Museum,
Virginia, on the age of exploration with timeline,
biographies, and activities.

www.nmm.ac.uk/Magellan
The National Maritime Museum, London, site with
a biography and details about Magellan's voyages
and the ships, seafarers, and life at sea of the time.

INDEX

Acknowledgments

We would also like to thank: Graham Rich, Val Garwood, John Guy, Peter Done, and Elizabeth Wiggans for their assistance, and David Hobbs for his map of the world. Picture research by Image Select.

NOTE TO READERS
The website addresses are correct at the time of publishing. However, due to the ever-changing nature of the Internet, websites and content may change. Some websites can contain links that are unsuitable for children. The publisher is not responsible for changes in content or website addresses. We advise that Internet searches should be supervised by an adult.